$15 LL

PHINEAS L. MACGUIRE . . .

GETS

SLIMED!

by FRANCES O'ROARK DOWELL • illustrated by PRESTON McDANIELS

Other books by Frances O'Roark Dowell

Phineas L. MacGuire . . . Erupts!
Chicken Boy
The Secret Language of Girls
Where I'd Like to Be
Dovey Coe

Houghton Mifflin Harcourt Edition

Printed in the United States of America

ISBN-13: 978-0-547-07387-3
ISBN-10: 0-547-07387-9

19 1083 15 14
4500473106

For Will Dowell, Boy Genius

—F. O. D.

The author would like to thank Tom and Kathryn Harris, next-door neighbors extraordinaire, for sharing their tale of the frog in the toilet. She would also like to thank Caitlyn Dlouhy, and Clifton and Jack Dowell, for their support and patience.

PHINEAS L. MACGUIRE . . .

GETS SLIMED!

△ chapter one

My name is Phineas Listerman MacGuire.

Most people call me Mac.

My Sunday-school teacher and my pediatrician call me Phineas.

A few people, mostly my great-uncle Phil and his cockatiel, Sparky, call me Phin.

Nobody calls me Listerman.

Nobody.

I mean not one single person.

Everybody got that?

I am currently in the fourth grade at Woodbrook Elementary School. On the first day of school my teacher, Mrs. Tuttle, asked us to write down our number one, two, and three goals for the year. Here is what I wrote:

1. To be the best fourth-grade scientist ever
2. To be the best fourth-grade scientist ever
3. To be the best fourth-grade scientist ever

So far this has not happened.

For example, I did not win the fourth-grade science fair. Me and my best friend, Ben, got an honorable mention.

We made a volcano. It was a pretty good volcano, since I am an expert volcano maker. But these days it takes more than baking soda and vinegar to get a science fair judge excited.

I learned that the hard way.

Today Mrs. Tuttle asked us to take out our goal sheets and review our goals. She says the first week of November is a good time for goal reviewing. She also says most people who don't meet their goals fail because they forget what their goals were in the first place.

"What is one step you can make this week that will help you meet one of your

goals?" Mrs. Tuttle asked. She took a yellow rubber frog from the jar of rubber frogs she keeps on her desk and balanced it on the tip of her finger. "Think of one small thing you can do."

I put my head down on my desk. After getting an honorable mention in the science fair, the only step I could take was to erase my three goals and start over. Maybe my goal could be to remember to take my gym clothes home on Friday afternoons.

Not that I would ever meet that goal either.

Aretha Timmons, who sits behind me in Mrs. Tuttle's class and who won second place in the fourth-grade science fair, popped her pencil against the back of my head.

"Why so glum, chum?" she asked.

"What goals did you put down, anyway?"

I held up my paper so she could read it. "Hmmm," she said. "Well, it's still pretty early in the year. You could do something amazing before Christmas if you put your mind to it."

Ben, who sits one row over and two seats back from me, leaned toward us. "I've got two words for you, Mac: Albert 'Mr. Genius Scientist' Einstein."

"That's five words," I said.

Maybe Ben's goal should be to learn how to count.

"My point is, Albert Einstein, the most

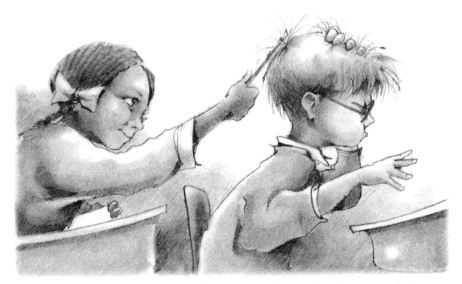

famous genius scientist of the world, flunked math about a thousand times. I don't think he even graduated from high school. He was a complete birdbrain until he was thirty or something."

"I didn't flunk math," I told him. "I just didn't win first prize at the science fair."

"See!" Ben shouted gleefully. "You're even smarter than Albert Einstein."

Ben is not a famous genius scientist, in case you were wondering.

He's a pretty good friend, though.

"What you need is a good project," Aretha said. "For example, if you could figure out a cure to a disease, that would be excellent. I've never heard of a fourth grader curing a disease before."

"Or maybe you could rid the world of mold," Ben said. "I mean, for a fourth grader, you sure know a lot about moldy junk."

It's true. I have always been sort of a genius when it comes to mold. Mold is like science that's happening all over your house, unless your family is really neat and tidy and cleans out the refrigerator on a regular basis.

This does not describe my family at all.

"Not all mold is bad," I told Ben, showing off my geniosity. "In fact, one of the most important medicines ever, penicillin, is made from mold."

"So figure out how to get rid of the bad mold," Ben said. "My mom would give you twenty bucks if you could get rid of the mold in our shower. That's all she ever talks about practically."

Rid the world of bad mold. It sounded

like the sort of thing a superhero would do in a comic book, if comic books were written by scientists with a special interest in single-celled organisms made out of fungus.

I could be Anti-Mold Man, Destroyer of Slime.

Not bad for a fourth grader.

I raised my hand. "Mrs. Tuttle, is it okay to change our goals, at least a little?"

"Revising your goals is a part of the process," Mrs. Tuttle said. "Sometimes we make goals that are unrealistic or not what we really want after all."

"Great!" I took out my pencil and started erasing my number one, two, and three goals. When I was done erasing, I wrote:

1. To get rid of all unnecessary mold in Woodbrook Elementary School
2. To teach Ben how to count
3. To be the best fourth-grade scientist ever

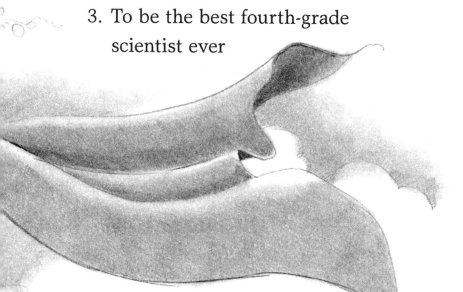

chapter two

Here is my routine after school is over: First I get off the bus and drag my backpack two blocks down the street to my house, which is located at 2505 Apple Blossom Road. The whole time I'm dragging my backpack, I'm thinking about what a dumb name Apple Blossom Road is, since not only are there no apple trees on my street, there are no other trees with blossoms either.

In fact, there are only seven trees on my street, and they are all oak trees.

The next street after my street is Cherry Tree Lane. Guess how many cherry trees there are?

I have no idea who thinks up this stuff.

After I finally get home, I open my front door and tiptoe to the kitchen, in case my sister, Margaret, who is two, is taking a nap. The last thing I want to do is to wake up Margaret, whose favorite

game is trying to fit her dolls' clothes over my head.

In case you were wondering, this is a very annoying game.

If it were up to me, I would go straight to my room the second I got home. My room is very comfortable. There are clothes everywhere, which gives it the lived-in look. I keep snacks in my underwear drawer and my top desk drawer, usually graham stick packs, snack-size potato chip bags, and chocolate pudding cups. My complete set of the Mysteries of Planet Zindar series is piled up next to my bed, so entertainment is not a problem.

In fact, I'm pretty sure if everyone else on the planet except me got sucked into a black hole, I could stay in my room and be fine for at least four months.

But I am not allowed to go straight to my room. There is a list of rules and regulations posted on our refrigerator, and under "After School," in the number one spot, is "Check in." So when I get home, I go to the kitchen, where I come face-to-face with the worst part of my day.

Her name is Sarah Fortemeyer.

She is the Babysitter from Outer Space.

Now, you would think, me being a scientist and everything, that I would like a space alien for a babysitter. Only, Sarah Fortemeyer is not the good kind of space alien—the kind who could tell you interesting facts about life on Mars, or who could give you lessons in advanced space alien laser beam technology.

No. She is a Teenage Girl Space Alien from the Planet of Really Pink Stuff.

"Hey, Macky Mac," she said the minute I walked into the kitchen today, the
same way she does every day. "Ready for
your snacky snack?"

I sighed. As a rule, I do not like sen-
tences that rhyme.

Especially when Sarah Fortemeyer
says them.

Sarah got up from the kitchen table
and began waving her fingers in the air.
For a second I thought she was trying to
put some Teenage Girl Space Alien spell

on me, but then I noticed the bottles of nail polish on the table.

"What do you think?" Sarah said, coming closer, her fingers still fluttering around. "Today I did three different colors: Ravishing Raspberry, Simply Summer Strawberry, and Green Day Green."

"No comment," I said.

I am a scientist. I do not have opinions on fingernail polish.

"Margaret really liked the Green Day Green, so I put some on her toes," Sarah said, walking over to the refrigerator. "You don't think your mom will mind, do you?"

My mom would probably throw a fit the size of Mount Vesuvius. She is not one of those go-with-the-flow kinds of moms you sometimes see on TV, moms who just sort of roll their eyes and laugh when their kids do some crazy stunt like pour hair dye on the dog's fur or draw pictures of pterodactyls on the living-room wall with permanent-ink markers.

My mom is a much more irritated mom than that.

I am sad to say, though, that she is under the spell of Sarah Fortemeyer and will not fire her, even if she did paint Margaret's toenails mucus green. This is because Sarah has her driver's license, always picks up Margaret from day care at exactly 2:45, and only charges five dollars an hour.

For five dollars an hour my mother has learned to live with things like green nail polish on Margaret's toes.

Sarah pulled a cup of strawberry yogurt from the fridge. "How 'bout some yogurt for a snack? It's nutritious and delicious!"

"You forgot that I'm allergic to yogurt," I said. "I would die from anaphylactic shock if that container even touched my skin."

"Your mom says you're allergic to nuts and cats, and that's all," Sarah said.

"My mom doesn't know all there is to know about me and my immune system," I said. "Besides, I'm not hungry. I'm going to go and do my homework."

That is Rule Number Two on the After School list: "Homework first!"

Which doesn't really make sense, since it's the second thing on the list. But when I pointed that fact out to my mom, she got her Mount Vesuvius look on her face and I decided maybe I shouldn't expect every-one to think in the same logical, rational way that me and my fellow scientists do.

"By the way, I tidied up your room for you," Sarah called as I went up the stairs. "Your mom said she'd pay me ten extra dollars if I did. And there's this really cute fuchsia scarf that I saw at Dillard's, so I need the money."

I sprinted upstairs. Sometimes Sarah acted like I was a fellow Teenage Girl Space Alien who was just dying to talk about clothes and makeup. If I didn't lock myself in my room, she'd go on and on about a bunch of girl stuff that would make me feel like I had cooties just by listening to it. It was information I didn't want anywhere near my brain.

As I opened my door, I closed my eyes, preparing myself for whatever was inside. With Sarah you get one of two kinds of room cleanings. Either you get the vacuum–dust–make the bed kind of cleaning, or you get the Teenage Girl Space Alien–Decides-to-Redecorate-Your-Room cleaning.

The second kind is the one you really want to avoid.

Fortunately, Sarah was not in a redecorating mood today, so mostly my room looked the same, only not so full of crumbs. And even I had to admit it was nice to have a little clear space on my desk so I could dump out my books from my backpack and not automatically lose them in a big pile of clutter.

A piece of paper followed my books out of my pack. Ben. Most people communicate through e-mail or instant messages or even the phone, but Ben communicates through comics. Ones he draws himself.

Ben is a genius artist. That's the only thing he's a genius at, but it makes up for all the rest of the stuff.

I unfolded the paper flat on my desk and read Ben's comic strip. In the first panel there was a picture of him sitting on his couch in front of the TV. A thought bubble said, "I'm bored!" He certainly did look bored.

In the second panel there was Ben again, only now a bunch of lightbulbs were going off all around his head.

In the third panel he was thinking, "I'll run for class president!"

And in the last panel he was holding up a picture of me. "But who will be my campaign manager? . . ."

I scrunched up the paper and threw it in the trash can. Ever since I'd known Ben, he'd had a bunch of really bad ideas, but running for class president had to be the worst. Here are the reasons:

1. To be elected class president, you either have to be someone like Stacey Windham, who is the right combination of mean and every once in a while nice, so that all the girls want to be her friend, or you have to be someone like Chester Oliphant, who is funny and pretty much everybody's favorite person in

the class. To be an annoying artistic genius like Ben is not going to win you any votes.

2. Ben would be a terrible president. He is unorganized and is always saying stuff that makes people mad, and he doesn't care about anything like school spirit or making the cafeteria ladies serve pizza every day instead of just on Fridays. All Ben cares about is drawing comic books.

3. I don't have time to be a campaign manager, and if Ben really wants to run for class president, he's going to need a campaign manager. But I have already dedicated my life to ridding Woodbrook Elementary

School of mold. This does not leave any room for politics.

That reminded me. I opened my door and yelled down the stairs, "Hey, Sarah, you didn't clean out the refrigerator today too, did you?"

"Yeah, I did," Sarah yelled back. "Your mom paid me twenty extra bucks to do that, which I really need because—"

I slammed my door shut. This was a real setback. Our refrigerator is one of the best sources of mold in the Western world.

I guessed I would have to go over to Ben's. Because if our refrigerator was the best source of mold, his bathroom shower was the second best. I could go over there, run some preliminary tests with different household cleaners, and start taking notes.

And while I was there, I would convince Ben that he'd win the Miss America contest before he'd win the class president election.

And he'd win by a lot more votes, too.

chapter three

"I'd make a great class president!"

Ben waved the remote at the TV set and let it do its magic. At my house we have a very strict TV-watching policy. You can only watch public-television cartoons, and then you can only watch the ones made for four-year-olds. At Ben's house you can choose from about fifty different cartoon networks, and on every single one someone is always either saying something really sarcastic or shooting some sort of computerized gizmo that makes everything explode.

It's awesome.

"Who told you you'd make a great class president?" I asked.

"My dad did," Ben said. "He called last night. He thinks I should start building my résumé."

"Fourth graders don't have résumés," I said.

Ben wagged his finger at me. "Fourth graders who aren't thinking about the future don't have résumés. My dad says it's never too early to start thinking about the future."

I flopped down on the couch. Ben's dad is a very tricky subject and not one you should tackle while you're standing up.

In my opinion, there are two not-so-great things about Ben's dad. One, he lives all the way in Seattle, Washington, since he and Ben's mom are divorced. Because he lives so far away, it is hard for him to come visit, and every once in a while Ben gets this dark, scowly look on his face, which means he is missing his dad and you better just leave him alone.

The second not-so-great thing about Ben's dad is that he is always trying to change who Ben is. He doesn't think boys should be artists. He tells Ben that he is going to have to change his mind about spending the rest of his life drawing comic books.

If you take comic-book drawing away from Ben, all you have is a person who sits there and watches TV in his pajamas.

"You know, if you become class president, you'll have to go to a lot of long, boring meetings with Principal Patino," I said. "And somebody like Stacey Windham will probably be vice president, and you'll have to call her on the phone every day to discuss class business. You will spend your entire life talking about school and thinking about school. You'll probably end up living at school."

Ben clicked off the TV and looked at me. His face was a very pale shade of green. "I've never heard of a kid having to live at school," he said.

"That's what happened last year," I told him. It was a big lie, but I was desperate. "You didn't go to our school then, so you wouldn't know about it, but all the class presidents ended up sleeping in the nurse's office practically every night."

I could see Ben was beginning to have second thoughts about running for class president. I sank back into the couch and smiled. My work was done.

Or maybe not.

"I'll just pass a law saying class presidents never have to stay after school, even if they get in trouble. It will be the big privilege of the class president to be able to leave school property whenever he wants to." Ben smiled and clicked the TV back on.

I rolled my eyes. "Yeah, like that's a law Mrs. Patino will approve in two seconds flat."

Ben shrugged. "The president makes the rules, what can I say?"

I could see this battle would not be won in an afternoon. I decided to turn my attention to mold.

Scientifically speaking, there are few things in the world more interesting than mold. Here's what I already knew, other than that mold is really gross in a cool kind of way:

1. Mold is a fungus. A fungus is a single-celled organism that grows into colonies of cells that become molds, mushrooms, and other cool stuff. Even though mold grows, it is not a plant or an animal. One way you know this is that no one wants it for a pet, and nobody wants to grow it in their garden, either.

2. Mold is everywhere. All you need is moisture, air, and stuff that mold likes to eat. If you look inside

my fridge, you will see that mold really, really likes cheese. But it likes other stuff too, like oranges that have been sitting out in a bowl on the kitchen table for a long time, and an old shoe box that maybe you one time tried to make sail like a boat in your bathtub and then stuffed into the cabinet under the bathroom sink when you heard your mom coming upstairs. Mold likes wet stuff a lot.

3. The way mold gets places is by sending out spores, which are kind of like seeds. If it is a dry kind of mold, the wind will blow its spores around for it. If it is a wet kind of mold, sometimes animals or insects will move it.

Slime molds, some of nature's most awesome organisms, move by sliming stuff. They just keep stretching along, eating anything in their path.

4. If you look at mold under a microscope, it looks a lot like spaghetti. Don't eat it!

   5. The mold that grows in your shower is called mildew. It is there because mold likes moisture.

Ben's shower is very, very moist.

When I pulled back the shower curtain, it was like I was interrupting a mildew party. Mildew was creeping up and down the walls and the shower curtain, and it was hanging around the drain like it couldn't wait for somebody to turn on some more water. The mildew was black and spotty and really, really cool looking.

In fact, it was so cool looking it occurred to me that I didn't actually want to get rid of it.

This was a problem.

"I guess we probably couldn't talk your mom into learning to live with mold, could we?" I asked Ben.

Ben shook his head. "No way. She hates it."

"If she really hated it, she'd get rid of it," I pointed out.

"She doesn't have time. And whenever she decides she's going to clean out the shower, it turns out she doesn't have the right supplies. It's a bad situation."

"But the mildew isn't actually hurting anything," I said. "Maybe if she tried to look at it in a more positive way, she wouldn't mind it so much. Maybe she could try to think of it as a sort of plant or something."

"It's slimy," Ben said. "It's gross and slimy, and you're pretty crazy if you think you're going to convince my mom to like it."

I knew Ben was right. But I also knew that deep down inside I wasn't a mold killer. I *like* mold. I think it's one of the most interesting things in the universe. If I start thinking about it, I come up with all sorts of fascinating questions, like is there mold in outer space? What is mold's favorite food? Does it like chocolate pudding cups as much as I do?

The more I thought about it, the more I knew I didn't want to rid the world of mold. What I really wanted was more mold. I wanted other people to be as interested in mold as I was so I'd have someone to discuss mold with. Maybe I should start a mold appreciation society or a club for mold lovers. I could be the president, and Ben could be vice president, if I could ever get him to like mold too.

Then we'd both have something to put on our résumés.

⚙ chapter four

My new and improved Fourth-
Grade Goal List:

1. To make everyone like
   mold as much as I do
2. To convince Ben not to run for
   class president
3. To be the best fourth-grade
   scientist ever

I knew that to get everybody else to like mold as much as I did, I would have to come up with some good mold publicity.

Scientifically speaking, Aretha Timmons was just the person to help me.

Normally, I am allergic to girls. I am allergic to thirteen things altogether, including nuts, cats, cottage cheese, grape jelly, and anything purple. Also kisses that come with lipstick attached, especially the kind my aunt Tiffany wears, which is not quite purple but close enough to make me break out in hives just thinking about it.

Aretha Timmons is the only girl I know that I am not 100 percent allergic to. I think it's because she is a fellow scientist and almost never wears purple. If we had to dissect a frog for fourth-grade science, Aretha would be the first person in line. She would not squeal or scream or cry because the frog was cute. She would get right down to business.

It's hard to be allergic to a girl like Aretha Timmons.

"Mold is a tough sell, Mac," she told me on the jungle gym at recess. "Number one, it's gross and slimy. Number two, nobody is ever excited to see mold."

"I am," I said.

"Yeah, Mac, but you're not like everyone else. Listen, last year in Ms. Perry's class, when we were cleaning out our desks for Spring Cleaning Day, Justin

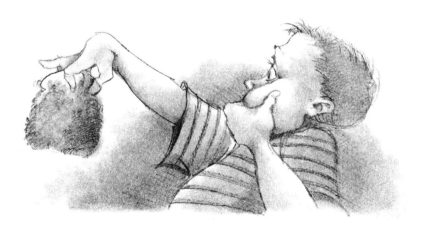

Fenner found a bologna sandwich in his desk that he'd forgotten about. It'd been in there for two months, and by Spring Cleaning Day it was just one big square of green mold. Do you think anyone said, 'Hey, pass that over here so I can see'? Do you think anyone asked to take it home to give to their mom for a present?"

"Well, no," I said. "But if Ms. Perry would have put the sandwich under a microscope and let everyone look at it, they would have seen how fascinating it was."

Aretha shook her head. "Ms. Perry screamed and ran to get Mr. Reid to come take Justin's desk out of the room. Ms. Perry was more grossed out than anybody."

"People like that should not be allowed

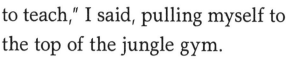

to teach," I said, pulling myself to the top of the jungle gym.

"It's true, we never did any interesting experiments in her class," Aretha said. "When it came to science, mostly we collected leaves."

"You know what would be cool?" I asked, dropping down to the ground. "A mold museum. It would be this place where all kinds of different molds were growing, like slime molds and mildew, and you could have information about everything so people would understand just how great mold really is."

Aretha nodded. "That's what you should do, then. You could ask Mrs. Tuttle if there's a shelf or something in her classroom.

Or else ask Mr. Reid if there's someplace in the basement you could use. I'll help you get set up. Mold doesn't bother me a bit."

Somehow I knew it wouldn't.

Mrs. Tuttle blew the whistle to let everyone know that recess was over. As I got closer to the building, I saw Ben standing on the steps, smiling a big, goofy fake smile and shaking hands with everybody in our class as they were about to walk through the door.

"What are you doing?" I asked him when I got to the front of the line.

"Running for president, just like I said I would," Ben said, shaking my hand. His hand was all sweaty. Who would vote for a kid with sweaty hands for president?

I mean, okay, I would, but only because he's my best friend.

"You've got to get over this idea," I said. "It won't work in a million years."

Ben flashed his fake grin at me. "Move along, move along, I've got more hands to shake."

I walked to Mrs. Tuttle's room. I was trying to feel excited about the mold museum idea, but instead I was feeling worried about Ben's running for president. The only thing Ben had ever won in his life was honorable mention for the fourth-grade science fair. He still had that dumb ribbon pinned to his backpack like it was the Nobel Prize in Physics, which is a very important award that the most genius scientists of all win.

If Ben lost the election—make that *when* Ben lost the election—he would probably be dark and scowly all the time, and then it wouldn't be fun to be best friends with him anymore. Only, I'd have to stay best friends with him, because otherwise it would seem like I'd stopped being best friends with him because he lost the election.

I was starting to feel sorry I lived in a democracy.

"I see the campaign for class president has already begun," Mrs. Tuttle said after everyone was back in their seats from recess. "Since Ben has gotten the ball rolling, let me see a show of hands from everyone who plans to run."

I looked around the classroom. Ben's hand was stretched a mile into the sky. Three seats behind him, Stacey Windham fluttered her hand in the air like a queen waving to all the little people. On the other side of the room, Chester Oliphant stuck his hand in the air, and so did Roland Forth, the only kid less likely to win than Ben.

Aretha popped her pencil on the back of my head. When I turned around, she nodded toward Ben. "That's not your idea, is it?" she asked.

"No," I said. "Do I look that dumb to you?"

"No, you don't," Aretha said. "Even Ben doesn't look that dumb to me. So why is he doing it?"

"It's his dad's idea."

Aretha rolled her eyes. She has a bossy dad too. "Well, his dad needs to wake up and smell the coffee, because Mr. Superhero Comic Book Man over there has a zero percent chance of winning this election."

I knew she was right. Everybody in the world knew she was right.

Everybody, that is, except for Ben.

And I had a feeling I wasn't going to be able to convince him that he was wrong.

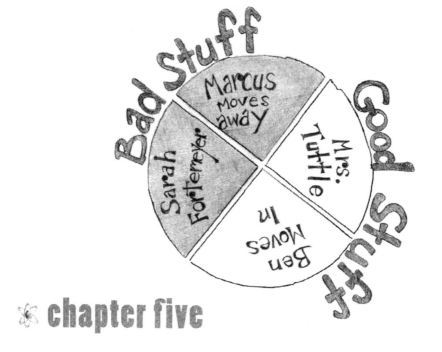

🔬 chapter five

Here is a scientific observation I have made about my life: For every good thing that happens, there is usually an equally bad thing that happens. For instance, this year I got Mrs. Tuttle for my teacher. That's a good thing. Then my mom hired Sarah Fortemeyer, Teenage Girl Space Alien, to be our babysitter. That's bad.

Very bad.

Sometimes it's the other way around,

though. At the beginning of the school year my best friend, Marcus, moved away, which was bad, but a little while later I got a new best friend, Ben, which was good.

At the end of every day you can add everything up to see how your life is going so far. If I graphed it, I think the graph would show that most days everything sort of evens out—not great, not terrible. At first I thought yesterday would be that kind of day. The mold museum idea was great, Ben running for president was not so great. It was kind of even steven. But then three things happened to make me change my mind:

1. At dinner my mom told me that she and my stepdad are going away this weekend. On Friday they are going to a dinner theater that's two hours away,

and coming home Saturday afternoon. At first I thought this was a great thing, because then maybe my dad could come and take care of me and Margaret, even if Margaret is my half-sister and not even related to him. My dad treats Margaret like she's a regular person. He doesn't even mind that she only says about seventeen words and is obsessed with this doll she has named Trudy, whose nose she has completely chewed off.

My dad just acts like Trudy is a regular person too.

"I'm sorry, but your father can't come this weekend," my mom told me when I asked if Dad would take care of us. "He's coaching the Mathletes again this year, and they've got a meet on Saturday."

"We could go there," I suggested. I love watching the Mathletes. My dad is a high school math teacher, and the Mathletes are his best students. My dad is a great teacher, so whenever I'm around his students, they treat me like I'm the world's most incredibly important person.

You could get used to being treated that way, in case you were wondering.

"I'm sorry, sweetie, but driving you to Dad's would take us three hours out of our way." My mom wiped her mouth with a Pete's Pizza Express napkin and smiled at me. "But I've got very exciting news. Guess who's going to take care of you while we're gone?"

"Grammy?"

I wouldn't mind if my grandmother took care of us. She's the only adult in captivity who actually believes watching TV is good for children.

"Even better! Sarah's going to babysit!"

My mother's smile stretched two miles wide, like she'd just told me she was giving me my own chemistry lab for Christmas.

I panicked. "Couldn't I stay at Ben's this weekend?" I asked.

"And miss the fun here? No way, mister!"

Sometimes when my mom is trying to convince you that something she wants you to do is a good idea, she gets this cheerful tone to her voice that is almost scary.

You would think that finding out Sarah the Teenage Girl Space Alien was staying at your house for an entire twenty-four-hour stretch, possibly longer, would be bad enough. You would not need one more negative thing in your life to make your day totally rotten. In fact, you would probably feel like another bad thing was entirely impossible.

You would be wrong.

2. After finding out about Sarah, I needed time to recover from the bad news and come up with a plan for keeping her away. So I went to my room to count my worms.

Counting worms is an excellent way to get your brain rolling.

I collect dried-up earthworms. So far I have 147, which I keep in a shoe box in my closet. The longest dried-up worm I have is four inches. My goal is to find one that is at least four feet. This will be hard to do because worms shrink up when they dry. Also, I will have to move to Australia to do this, since they have the longest worms.

I asked my mom if we could move to Australia, but she said no.

I asked my stepdad, Lyle, if we could move to Australia, and he said maybe, and if we didn't move there, maybe we could take a vacation there someday.

If you have to have a stepdad, Lyle is the kind to get.

When I got up to my room, I couldn't find the shoe box. Usually if something gets lost in my closet, it's because it's gotten mixed up with a bunch of my shirts and pants, which I'm supposed to hang up, only I never do. In case you're wondering, if you pile stuff up just right, it hardly wrinkles at all.

I went to look for the shoe box under a pile of clothes, but all of a sudden I realized that there wasn't a pile of clothes. All my clothes were hanging from hangers.

All my shoes were lined up in a row on the closet floor.

All my games and LEGOs and Lincoln Logs were stacked up neatly.

Sarah the Teenage Girl Space Alien had cleaned my closet.

"Mom!" I yelled at the top of my lungs. "Sarah threw out my worms!"

I ran to check the outside garbage cans. No shoe box. I checked the recycling bin. No shoe box.

"Sarah probably dropped it off at Goodwill," my mom said when I came back into the house. "I asked her to pull out all the clothes in your closet that didn't fit anymore. She probably just looked at the size printed on the shoe box and thought there were too-small shoes in there."

"She should have looked in the box!

Who takes a shoe box to Goodwill without even looking to see what's inside? It could have been a box full of tarantulas!"

"She would have heard tarantulas scurrying around inside the box," my mom pointed out.

I should mention that my mom is not the world's biggest fan of my dried-worm collection. Which probably explains why she didn't sound too upset about the missing shoe box.

I sat down on the couch and put my head in my hands. Two years of worm collecting, down the drain.

My mom must have realized how depressed I was. "I'll call Goodwill tomorrow and see if they've found your worms," she said. "I'm sure they would be more than happy to return them."

I decided to go to bed so that no more

bad stuff could happen to me. Usually you're pretty safe in bed.

Except when you remember you have a book report that is due first thing in the morning.

3. I had my pajamas on, my teeth brushed, the light turned off, and was chewing on a Fruit Roll-Up I'd found under my pillow, when I remembered. One page, front and back, every other line, whatever book I wanted. Plot summary and personal analysis.

No copying off the book jacket.

I sighed. Every time Mrs. Tuttle assigned us a book report, I always meant to do a really good job. I was going to read a book and write the report the minute I finished. It would be a book I had never read before, and I would make many interesting observations.

It is a known fact that most scientists are excellent book report writers.

Only, I never got around to reading a book I had never read before. This is because there are forty-three books in the Mysteries of Planet Zindar series, and I keep reading them over and over.

I am obsessed with the planet Zindar.

I leaned over and picked up book number twenty-four from the stack of Planet Zindars beside my bed. *The Red Monster Returns*. I started reading it, just to refresh my memory.

And then I fell asleep.

◎ chapter six

This morning when I woke up, *The Red Monster Returns* was on top of my face, making it sort of hard to breathe. My bedside lamp was still on. My book report had not been written. I was pretty sure I was starting the second bad day in a row.

And then something awesome happened.

It all started when I had to go to the bathroom.

"At first I thought the frog in the toilet was dead," I told everybody in Share and Stare later. Share and Stare is what Mrs. Tuttle has instead of Show and Tell. In Share and Stare you are only allowed to talk about stuff that has to do with what we're studying in Mrs. Tuttle's class. Like, if you found a Froot Loop in the shape of Alaska, and we were studying U.S. geography, you could bring that in. Or if your aunt sent you a postcard of a giraffe when we were studying vertebrates in science, that would be a good thing to share.

You are not allowed to share your stuffed pig named Oinky just because you feel like it, which Roland Forth learned the hard way.

"I knew it was a frog right away and not a toad," I said, "because it had really long legs. You could tell it was a frog that had been a really good jumper. So that made me feel extra bad that it was dead. Only, it wasn't dead at all, which I found out when my sister, Margaret, ran in and tried to flush it down the toilet."

You would not have believed how far that frog jumped.

I mean, it went at least eight feet.

Right on top of my mom's head.

Okay, it really landed right on top of her shoulder, but that doesn't make as good of a picture as a frog landing on

her head. Which it almost did, but it lost its balance at the last minute and plopped onto her shoulder instead.

Have I mentioned that my mom does not like frogs?

"Mac!" she screamed. "Get this monster off me! Now!"

"It's not a monster, Mom," I explained. "It's an amphibian. That means it lives part of its life in water and part of its life on land."

"I don't care if it lives part of its life on Neptune," my mom yelled. "Get it out of here!"

By this time the frog had jumped off my mom's shoulder and was hopping down the stairs.

"Neptune's too cold," I told my mom as I ran down the stairs after the frog. "Besides, it's a gaseous planet, so it'd be pretty hard to hop around on."

I always enjoy it when you can bring interesting scientific knowledge into everyday conversation.

Right as the frog hit the landing, my stepdad came in through the front door with the morning paper. In came Lyle, out went the frog. In about three hops he was across our front yard and heading for the street. He hit the curb just as Markie Vollencraft was speeding by in his VW Bug with the window down.

One last hop and that frog was in the VW Bug and headed straight for West Linnett High School.

I am not making this up.

Mrs. Tuttle gave me a look like she thought I was. "That must have been quite some hop, Mac," she said.

"Frogs can jump over twenty times their own length," I told her. I'd taken the *F–He* volume of our old encyclopedia set with me to read on the bus, so I was

filled with frog information. "That would be like you or me jumping a hundred feet. The longest recorded frog jump is thirty-three feet and five inches. Compared to that, my frog jumping into Markie Vollencraft's VW Bug was nothing."

"So how'd the frog get in the toilet?" Brandon Woo asked.

"That's what I'm not sure about," I said. "Maybe it came through the pipes. But I don't know if a frog could do that or not."

"You should ask Mr. Reid," Aretha said. "I bet he knows a lot about pipes."

Mr. Reid is our school janitor. He is famous for being able to fix anything, including the sinks in the boys' bathrooms, which for some mysterious reason are always getting clogged up with soggy toilet paper, and the school's field trip van, which breaks down at least once during every field trip. The teacher in charge always carries Mr. Reid's cell phone number so she can call him from wherever the van has broken down and he can come and make it run long enough to get back to school.

That's how I ended up going down to the basement to talk to Mr. Reid at lunch. In fact, Mrs. Tuttle made me go, since by that time all anybody in my class could talk about was how that frog could have gotten into my toilet.

"I'd say it'd be unusual for a frog to

make it all the way up through the pipes," Mr. Reid told me when I explained to him what had happened that morning. He stroked his chin, like he was giving the matter some serious thought. "Where would a frog get into the system and swim up? Did he swim through the sewage line? Not unless there was a broken place where he could've gotten in. But if you've got a broken place in the sewage line, you've got sewage coming out of the sewage line, if you dig what I'm saying."

I shook my head. I didn't dig.

"Sewage, son," Mr. Reid said, "is what we flush down the toilet. Goes into the sewage pipes running underground, all the way to the treatment plant. Believe you me, sewage gets out through an open pipe, you'll hear about it pronto. But you'll smell it first."

Mr. Reid took a bite of his ham sandwich. I was wondering how he could eat during a conversation about sewage, but I guess if you're a janitor, you probably get used to gross stuff. It might not affect you at all after a while.

"My guess is that frog got into the house through the door, same way it got out," Mr. Reid continued. "Maybe it hopped in on its own, maybe it was in a box or a bag."

Realizing that Mr. Reid didn't seem at all bothered by sewage, I decided now would be a good time to bring up my mold museum idea. I'd already asked Mrs. Tuttle about making a mold museum in the science corner of our room, but she'd said she was pretty sure the state health department had rules about growing mold in classrooms.

To be honest, she looked a little green when I told her my mold museum idea in the first place. It made me realize how much everyone, even teachers, needs to be educated about mold.

"A basement is an ideal place for it," I explained to Mr. Reid after I'd told him my basic plan, "since it's naturally damp."

Mr. Reid nodded. "It's the moisture from the earth seeping in through the walls," he said. "The only problem is, there's not much natural light in here. Some molds like a little light."

I stared at Mr. Reid. "You know about mold?" I asked. "I mean, real facts about mold?"

Mr. Reid grinned. "Sure I know about mold. You ever heard of Alexander Fleming?"

"He discovered penicillin," I said. I was almost whispering, I was so surprised to be having a two-way scientific conversation about mold. This had never happened to me before.

"That's right," Mr. Reid said. "He was growing bacteria in a petri dish, and some mold got in there."

"And the mold killed the bacteria!"

Me and Mr. Reid slapped high fives.

"You get Mrs. Patino's permission, and

you can have your museum down here," Mr. Reid told me. "I think mold is pretty interesting stuff myself."

I shook my head. I had known Mr. Reid since kindergarten, and this was the first time I'd realized he was a scientific genius.

It's pretty cool that there are two of us in the same school.

chapter seven

This afternoon, after school, I rode the bus home with Ben. I needed his artistic-genius help with my mold museum presentation for Mrs. Patino. In return I promised I'd help him work on his campaign strategy.

The best strategy I could come up with was that Ben should drop out of the race. Immediately.

"Can't do it," Ben said. We were sitting

on the floor of his bedroom. Ben was working on a new comic book, and I was drawing mold samples in my notebook, using colored pencils. "My dad said if I win, he'll come visit and stay for the whole weekend, all the way till Monday morning. We'll stay at a hotel and watch pay-per-view and eat pizza."

"He could do that even if you didn't run for class president," I pointed out.

"No, because he has to take off work to come visit, so it's easier for me to go see him. Him coming here is special."

Ben held up his sketch pad so I could see how the story was coming along. In the comic-book series he's doing, his main guy, Derek the Destroyer, races around the globe saving the world from evil. In this story Derek was thwarting an amazon girls' volleyball team in their

attempt to take over the White House and force everyone in the country to play volleyball twenty-four hours a day.

Volleyball, in case you were wondering, is not exactly Ben's favorite sport.

"That's cool about your dad coming here," I said. "But you've got to be realistic about the election. Why would somebody vote for you instead of Chester or Stacey?"

Ben chewed on his pencil. "Because I'm a good artist?"

"That's all you've got?" I asked. "Why should anybody vote for you just because you're an artist?"

"I'm a creative guy," Ben said. "Creative people are creative problem solvers, Mrs. Tuttle said so."

"So, what problems are you going to solve?"

"I've been thinking about that," Ben

said. "Have you ever noticed that around ten thirty everybody's stomachs start growling? But there's still an hour until lunch, and you can't concentrate on anything because you're, like, totally starvazoid."

"Starvazoid" is one of Ben's made-up words. He practically has his own dictionary of Ben words that sound like they just jumped out of a stack of comic books.

"So, what's your idea?" I asked. "Mandatory snack time?"

"Exactly!" Ben exclaimed. "It doesn't have to be anything fancy. I'm thinking doughnuts and milk, maybe, or candy bars."

I thought about this for a few seconds. "It's got to be nutritious," I told him. "Definitely no candy. But overall it's not a bad idea. You could be onto something here."

Ben grinned. "Okay, then, check out this cool-a-bomb idea. Two words, buddy: mucho, mucho longer recess."

"That's four words."

"Two words, four words, same dif," Ben said. "My point is, we get fifteen lousy minutes on the playground after lunch. By the time you choose up teams for kickball, you have, like, three minutes to play the game."

"But you hate playing kickball," I said. "Today you spent recess trying to build a T. rex out of broken Popsicle sticks."

"It's not about me," Ben said. "It's about the people."

I had to admit, the people would definitely vote for more recess.

"Those are good ideas," I told him.

"But you've still got a problem. Chester and Stacey are really popular. You're, well, less popular."

"I know," Ben said. "I still haven't figured how to creatively solve that problem."

We decided to work on my mold presentation. Sometimes if you stop thinking about something for a while, you get an awesome idea without even trying. It's like all the neurons in your brain just keep popping away all by themselves until they hit on the exact right thing.

The brain, in case you were wondering, is an incredible machine.

I showed Ben this killer mold book I'd checked out of the library. "I figured

I could write down a lot of interesting facts about mold, and then you could copy them over on a poster and draw some good pictures. I mean, pictures that make the mold look really amazing. Like art, practically."

Ben nodded. "I could do that," he said. "In the close-up pictures mold isn't nearly half so gross looking as it looks in real life. You could probably fool Mrs. Patino into thinking that mold is something really cool. Like something she might want to give someone for Christmas."

That was probably taking things too far. Nobody likes mold more than I do, but I still don't want to find it in my stocking on Christmas morning.

Still, I was glad Ben was finally on Team Fungus.

Ben started sketching out pictures of

mold on a piece of poster board, while I wrote down fascinating mold facts, such as:

1. We eat mold! Lots of cheeses are naturally moldy — Camembert and blue cheese get their flavor from molds, *Penicillium camemberti* and *P. roqueforti,* to be exact.
2. Slime molds move! It's how they get their food—they sort of creep over rotten stuff, like old logs or leaves, then surround it and eat the bacteria that's growing there.

3. A bunch of slime molds are named after foods, including tapioca slime, pretzel slime, scrambled-egg slime, raspberry slime, and cotton-candy slime.

It only took an hour to come up with an amazing poster presentation. Ben drew four of the most beautiful molds known to humankind: *Ceratiomyxa fruticulosa*, otherwise known as white coral slime; *Pulcherricium caeruleum*, which is blue and sort of velvety; *Licea sambucina*, a slime mold made up of really tiny orange balls; and another slime mold, *Lamproderma granulosum*, that looks like greenish soap bubbles.

There's probably nothing more beautiful on the whole planet Earth than a colorful slime mold.

Mrs. Robbins, Ben's mom, stuck her head in the doorway. She manages the apartment complex where she and Ben live, and when she's working, she always calls from the office or comes by every thirty minutes or so to check on Ben and make sure he isn't getting into trouble.

About 85 percent of the time he is.

"What's that?" she asked, pointing to Ben's mold pictures. "It's really beautiful. Like flowers, almost, but not quite. Under-sea plants, maybe?"

"It's mold," Ben said, coloring in some *P. caeruleum* with a blue Magic Marker.

Ben's mom put her hand over her mouth like Ben had just told her he was drawing dog poop. "No way!"

"Yep!" Ben grinned. "It's for Mac's big science project."

I could tell he was starting to enjoy

the way that just talking about mold could freak some people out.

Ben's mom shook her head. "Comic books and mold. You boys make quite a team."

After his mom left, Ben got quiet for a minute. Ben is always quiet when he's drawing, but when he's not drawing, usually he's talking. In fact, it's pretty hard to shut him up. So when he's quiet and not drawing, watch out.

When he suddenly jumped on his bed and started dancing around, I knew I was in serious trouble.

"I just came up with a fantastatomic plan!" he yelled, like I was in Alaska instead of sitting five feet away from him. "Why don't you run for vice president on my presidential ticket? You could pick out the snacks every day if you

VOTE FOR BEN

FOR CLASS PRESIDENT

AND
MAC

wanted to, and you could be in charge of punishing the people who rebel against our administration!"

I thought about this plan for approximately three seconds. To be honest, I didn't actually need three seconds to know the answer was no. I am a scientist, not a politician.

But right as I was about to open my mouth and deliver the bad news, I had one of my famous Big Mac attacks. I could not believe my own personal geniosity at that very moment.

My brain had come through, just like I knew it would.

"I'm not the one you need to run as your vice president," I told Ben. "But I know who is."

✿ chapter eight

"Forget it."

Aretha popped her pencil on her desk about ten times, like she wanted us to understand how serious she was about saying no.

"Number one," she said, "I have no interest in politics. Number two, I am much too busy with extracurricular activities, such as trombone lessons, Girl Scouts, and soccer. And number three,

I am not the vice presidential type."

Aretha had a point. She is not exactly the sort of person who takes orders from other people.

Especially other people like Ben.

"I'll trade you something for it," Ben said, leaning over from his desk. "I could do an awesome drawing of you. A vice presidential portrait. They could hang it in the principal's office. Or you could give it to your mom for Christmas."

For a minute it looked like Aretha was considering this. Having a good drawer offer to draw a picture of you is hard to turn down. Also, it's a bonus not to have to figure out what to give your mom for Christmas. A couple of years ago, for example, I couldn't think of anything to give my mom. I ended up buying her a big jar of red wiggler worms so

she could compost all of our trash in a bucket under the kitchen sink.

Scientifically speaking, this explains the humongous population of red wiggler worms that now live in the dirt out by our swing set.

But Aretha turned Ben's offer down. "Can't do it," she said. "The election is at the end of next week. There's no way you could get enough support to win by then, even if I was on your ticket."

Ben chewed on his pencil. He got a very sad expression on his face.

It was his fake sad expression, but Aretha didn't know that.

"Fine," Ben said. "I guess I'll just drop out of the race, then. I can't win without somebody like you, a person that everybody likes and respects and admires, on my ticket." He sighed. "I guess I'll just call my dad tonight and tell him that I'll be letting him down."

Aretha looked at Ben. "Does it really matter to your dad that much?"

Ben nodded. "It's what's keeping him alive. See, he's got this mysterious illness—"

I cut Ben off. "What Ben is saying is that his dad has been sort of down in the dumps lately. Ben's campaign is keeping his mind off of his troubles."

That was a lie too, but it was less of a lie than Ben's lie about his dad's mysterious illness.

"My dad's depressed," Ben said. "He got fired from his job last week."

Great. Lie number three.

"How come?" Aretha asked.

"He stole a hundred thousand dollars from the cash register."

"Your dad worked at a place where they keep a hundred thousand dollars in the cash register?"

"Uh-huh," Ben said. "He works at a bank. He's a bank teller."

"He's a bank teller and he stole a hundred thousand dollars? And all they did was fire him?" Aretha asked.

"His trial is in two weeks," Ben said. "That's the other reason he's so depressed."

Aretha shook her head. "I know you are making this story up, Ben. I know you are trying to make me feel sorry for

you. Well, I guess your plan has worked, because I feel sorry for anybody who has to make up a bunch of lies just to get somebody else to help him out. That's pathetic."

"I know," Ben admitted. "But I thought it was worth a try."

Aretha straightened up in her seat. "Here is the deal. I will run as the vice presidential candidate on your ticket, but I want something in return."

She turned to me. "I want you to help me make penicillin."

"Penicillin? Me?" I asked. "Why? Can't your doctor give you a prescription?"

"It's for a Girl Scout merit badge," Aretha said. "It's called A Healthier You. What's healthier for you than penicillin?"

"I don't know the first thing about how to make penicillin," I said.

Ben leaned over and punched me on the shoulder. "Come on, Mac! You could figure it out. Just buy a kit off the Internet or something!"

"What do you say, Mac? It's a hard-to-beat deal. I'll help out your friend if you'll help me out."

I sighed. "I guess we could try. But isn't there an easier way for you to get a merit badge?"

"I don't do things the easy way," Aretha said. "I do them the Aretha way."

Then she turned to Ben and held up her hand. They slapped high fives. "Okay, Ben," she said, "we've got a lot of work to do."

They had a lot of work to do? What about me? I had to figure out how to make penicillin, the most important medical invention of the twentieth century.

In case you were wondering, penicillin production is not a normal part of the fourth-grade science curriculum.

Unless you are Aretha Timmons.

⚛ chapter nine

Here is the list of everything I have to get done this weekend:

1. Write a speech for Ben for the Meet the Candidates session on Monday. This was part of the deal Aretha made with us. If she had to be Ben's vice presidential running mate, I had to be Ben's speechwriter. Ben may be a

genius artist, but he can't write his way out of a box filled with dictionaries and all the famous speeches of the universe.

2. Begin developing sample molds to show Mrs. Patino for our big Mold Museum meeting on Tuesday.

3. Write the book report I never got around to writing for Mrs. Tuttle.

4. Make penicillin. And maybe when I am finished, I can reinvent the cure for polio.

But before I got started on my list of things to do, I had to go with Sarah Fortemeyer, Teenage Girl Space Alien babysitter, to Goodwill to get my worms back.

Sarah was waiting for me in the driveway when I got home from school on

Friday. She was leaning against my mom's minivan, jingling the keys. My mom and Lyle had taken Lyle's car on their trip, leaving the van for Sarah in case there was an emergency situation.

"Hop in the van, Stan," she said. "The Goodwill people called five minutes ago. Somebody found your worms when they were sorting through clothing donations. Lucky for us, the manager your mom talked to was working, so he called right away."

This was the best news I'd heard all week. It almost made up for having to spend twenty-four hours straight with Sarah Fortemeyer.

Almost, but not quite.

"Let's go!" I yelled. I threw my back-pack on the front steps and jumped in the van. Margaret was already in her car seat and looking at her favorite *Monkey Makes a Milk Shake.*

Before I became a scientist, *Mr. Monkey* was my favorite book too.

This is not something I advertise.

For a Teenage Girl Space Alien, Sarah Fortemeyer is an okay driver. The only problem about being in the van with her is that she has this sort of purple smell, which is either her perfume or her natural Teenage Girl Space Alien scent. Either way it makes me itchy. Fortunately, we made it to Goodwill before my body broke out in red, scratchy hives. My weekend was already going to be rotten. There was no need to add hives to the mix.

When I got my worms back at Goodwill, ten of them were missing. "They must have fallen out of the box when the lid was taken off," the manager said. He shrugged, like ten missing dried worms was no big deal.

To me, it was a big deal.

Do you know how hard it is to find dried worms? Oh, maybe if you live in Australia, it's not a problem. But where I live, finding a dried worm is a major event. Especially if it's not smushed beyond recognition.

"I've got to find those worms!" I said. "They're scientifically important to me and to worm collectors everywhere!"

"I'm sorry," the manager said. "Only Goodwill employees are allowed in the sorting areas."

"You don't understand!" I yelled, but the manager just shook his head. You could tell he wasn't going to budge.

"Don't worry about it, Mac," Sarah said. "I personally guarantee that I'll find you ten worms this weekend to make up for the ones you lost."

"Dried worms?" I asked.

Sarah nodded. "Dried worms."

"Okay," I said. At least that would keep Sarah out of my hair. She'd have to spend the whole weekend searching high and low.

It has been a bad fall for dried worms.

When we got home, Sarah immediately turned on the TV to some talk show. I thought about watching, just because I never get to watch anything at my house besides *Polly Puppy and Her Puppy Friends*. But after one minute I learned a valuable lesson.

There are some shows even stupider than *Polly Puppy*.

I know. It's hard to believe.

Besides, I needed to make some penicillin, and fast. Aretha said if I didn't have something growing by Monday, she wouldn't put her name on Ben's presidential ticket.

"I need to use the computer," I told Sarah. "I have some scientific research to do."

"Are you allowed to use the computer, Scooter?" Sarah asked. "I thought your mom had a 'No computer' rule."

"Actually, it's a 'No computer on school days until after dinner, and then only if all homework has been completed

and all teeth have been brushed' rule," I explained. "Besides, my mom has about two million filters downloaded. It's not like I can actually do anything fun on the computer."

"Okay," Sarah said. "As long as you can't have any fun, I guess that's all right."

Sarah Fortemeyer and my mom are two peas in a pod.

I sat down at the computer on my mom's desk in the family room and typed "penicillin" in a search engine. In about two seconds I got a return of 6,140,000 hits.

Maybe I would need to narrow my search specifications.

I typed in "How to grow penicillin."

I got 550,000 hits.

That would have to do.

The first thing I learned was that to make penicillin, you have to grow a mold called penicillium. Penicillium produces a liquid that is made into penicillin. All I needed was a lemon, a milk carton, and some dust.

In our house finding dust would not be a problem.

The lemon and the milk carton, on the other hand, would take a little more work.

I stuck my head in the fridge. I found a half-full plastic milk jug with no lid and not one single lemon. There was a carton of smushy, oozing cherry tomatoes, three chunks of cheddar just beginning to show green spots, and something in a plastic container that I couldn't recognize. There was even a plastic lemon that at one time had held lemon juice but was now empty. But no real lemons or citrus fruit of any kind.

We would have to go to the store. That meant another car trip with the Teenage Girl Space Alien. Which meant more purple smells. More potential for red, scratchy hives breaking out all over my body.

I picked up the phone and called Ben. "You have to help me," I said. "I need a lemon and a milk carton, and I need them fast."

"No prob," Ben said. "I'll be there in ten minutes, tops."

chapter ten

Forty-five minutes later Ben showed up at my front door.

He had two plastic bags dangling from his bike handles. In one there were three cartons of milk. Full cartons.

In the other there were about forty lemons.

"The great thing about living in an apartment complex is that somebody always has what you need," Ben said, carrying the bags into the house. "Especially when about nine out of ten people who live there are senior citizens. Senior citizens have the best supplies. They're totally organized."

"Why'd you get so much stuff?" I asked. "I mean, one lemon and one empty milk carton would have done it."

"Yeah, I know," Ben said. "Only, when Mrs. Markowitz heard that Mrs. Grimes was giving me a lemon, she swore she had an even better lemon, and Mr. Penderthal said he had the best lemons of all. It went on like that for about twenty minutes."

"Well, all we need is one little lemon wedge," I said.

Ben thought about this for a second. "Maybe we can donate the rest to charity," he said.

We spent the next ten minutes drinking milk and eating cookies. Then I washed out the empty milk carton and sliced a lemon wedge.

"Step one," I said, "is putting dust on the lemon."

I swiped the lemon wedge on top of our fridge. It came back loaded with dust.

"Step two," I said, "the lemon wedge goes in a plastic Baggie, and we add five drops of water."

"And step three," I said after I'd put the lemon wedge in the bag and Ben had used an eyedropper to drop five drops of water in with it, "is putting the Baggie in the milk carton and sealing the carton."

"How long will it take the penicillin to grow?" Ben asked.

"A few days, I think," I told him. "I'll

put the milk carton in the bathroom closet so it can get nice and steamy."

Ben looked thoughtful. "You know, this science stuff is pretty cool. Not as cool as art, but almost."

"I'm glad you think so," I told him. "Because we've got a lot more work to do."

There was mold to be made. Lots of mold.

Really, when you think about it, it was my kind of Friday night.

"Mold experiment number one," I said, "bread mold. The world's most common mold, some would say. All we need is a slice of bread, a plastic Baggie, and some water."

"I get to do the water drops again!" Ben yelled.

"Okay," I told him. "You're good at that."

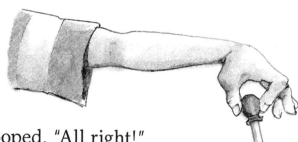

Ben whooped. "All right!"

Sometimes it is ridiculously easy to make him happy.

The first trick was finding some bread in my house that wasn't already moldy. Finally I noticed an unopened bag of white bread in a cabinet that looked relatively mold-free. I took out a slice, and Ben dribbled some water on it.

"Now we leave the bread exposed to the air for about thirty minutes, pop it in the Baggie, put it in a closet, and wait for the mold to start growing. We ought to see something in three or four days."

"And then what do we do?" Ben asked.

"Just look at it," I said. "Just admire the wonder and beauty that is mold."

"So we don't have to eat it or anything, right?"

"No way," I said. "In fact, you're not even supposed to ever open the bag again. Some people are allergic to mold spores, so you don't want to let any out of the bag. Everything has to be destroyed."

"That is so cool," Ben said.

Next I found a nearly empty mayonnaise jar in the fridge. "We'll clean this out and use it for our mold terrarium. We'll put in four or five different kinds of food, spray on a little water, put on the lid, and wait for the fun to begin."

Ben and I looked through the refrigerator and the cabinets and came up with one tomato slice, a piece of cheese, half a stale chocolate-covered doughnut, a handful of Cheerios, and a clump of macaroni. I turned the jar on its side and put the different foods inside. Ben added the water. "I can't wait until all this mold starts growing," he said. "It's just going to be like this zoo of fungus."

That's when inspiration hit me. "Maybe we could jump-start it," I said. "Give our mold experiments a steam bath to get them growing. Only, if we do it in my bathroom, Margaret will destroy everything."

Ben frowned. "I'd say let's do it at my place, but my mom would just scream and throw everything out."

And that's when I had inspiration number two. "But my mom's not here.

Her bathroom's going to be empty until tomorrow night. We can put all the mold up there now, run a hot shower for thirty minutes, turn off the water, close up the doors, and let the steam do its magic. Who'll know the difference?"

"Excellent idea!" Ben exclaimed.

It took us only a few minutes to transport all our mold experiments upstairs and get the steam bath going. Once my mom's bathroom was nice and steamy, I shut off the water and shut the door behind us. "All right, then," I said when we were back downstairs. "This is a good start. But the best part of our mold project is yet to come."

"Better than spraying water on everything?" Ben asked.

"A hundred times better," I told him. "A million billion times better."

Ben's eyes got wide. "What is it?"

"I think you better plan on spending the night," I told him. "Because in the morning we're going on a slime hunt."

chapter eleven

The amazing thing to me about science
is that it is everywhere.

It is a lot like mold in that way.

I mean, look around you. There is dirt,
water, and air. There is the sun and grav-
ity. There are chemical reactions happening all over the place. Baking cookies is
a scientific activity. Pour a little vinegar
on some baking soda, and you get an
explosion.

I mean, how cool is that?

And if you're reading a great book about slime mold, and you get all excited and start wishing like anything you could see some slime mold for yourself, you don't have to book the next flight to Australia. You can go out to the woods behind your house and find your very own slime mold right where you live.

This idea is more exciting to some people than to others.

"You're going out to the woods to do what?" Sarah Fortemeyer asked Saturday morning when me and Ben announced we were off on an important scientific expedition.

"To find some slime molds," I told her again.

"The slimiest slime molds that ever lived," Ben added.

"And this is something that would be okay with your mom?"

"My mom understands the importance of scientific discovery," I said. I wasn't really making that up, either. It's true my mom doesn't like messes, and she pretty much hates frogs and almost any kind of insect you can think of. She has no appreciation for smelly stuff. I've asked for a chemistry set for every birthday and Christmas for the last three years, but so far her answer has been a big fat N-O. In general, she doesn't like me doing anything that has the potential to mess up her carpet or burn down the house.

But she takes me to the science museum downtown every other Sunday afternoon and whenever they open a new exhibit, and even though she complains about the mess I make when I start a new scientific project, she never says I can't do it.

It's possible that in secret my mom kind of wishes she were a scientist herself.

The woods behind my house would not appear to be the best woods in the world for scientific research, but even the smallest ecosystem is filled with surprises.

"Look for rotten stuff," I told Ben as we walked through my backyard. "Tree bark on the ground. Wet, rotted wood. Dead leaves."

It hardly took any time at all to find a nice slab of yellow slime mold growing on a chunk of wet pine bark.

"It looks like somebody threw up," Ben observed.

"Pretty cool, huh?"

"The coolest," Ben said.

"Here's my idea," I said as I carefully put the bark in a large bread bag. "We get a couple of these babies and we have a slime mold race. Keep track of which slime is sliming the fastest, that sort of thing."

"You know, this is giving me a great idea for a new comic book," Ben said, handing me another piece of slimy bark. *Slime Man*—'Don't Look Now, But You're About to Get Slimed!'"

Don't ever let anyone tell you science does not get the creative juices flowing.

The last thing we did was collect

some slime-free bark. The night before I'd read about an experiment where you could make your own slime mold in a plastic container. I could hardly get to sleep thinking about it—I could grow slime mold in my very own room.

All you have to do to grow your own slime mold is put a piece of paper towel in a plastic container, place some bark on top, cover the bark with water, and cover the container with plastic. Next day you dump out the water and re-cover the container. You have to wait a few weeks, but eventually you'll have slime mold growing in your room, your bathroom, on top of your TV, wherever you feel like.

By the end of the morning we had everything we needed for the start of an excellent mold museum, if not an entire mold empire.

Now all I had to do was everything else. Come up with a speech for Ben and pound out my overdue book report. After Ben left, I went up to my room to get to work. Just as I was about to write the first line of the speech—something brilliant, like "Hello, my name is Ben Robbins, and I am running for president of Mrs. Tuttle's fourth-grade class"—there was a knock on my door.

Just what I needed, a visit from Sarah Fortemeyer, Teenage Girl Space Alien. "Go away, I'm busy!" I yelled.

"I've got something I think you'll want to see," Sarah singsonged through my closed door.

"I doubt it," I said. She was probably just dying to show me her whole collection of fingernail polish, a million bottles of Dust Bowl Orange and Atomic Raygun

Red, Putrid Pink Peonies and Wilted Wildflowers.

Actually, for nail polish, that stuff didn't sound so bad.

It's when they call it Purple Passionflower that a scientist has got to keep his guard up.

"I mean it, Mac," Sarah said. "You won't believe what I found."

She'd probably gone through my mom's bottom dresser drawer, the one where my mom keeps scarves and feathery and furry things. It's the stuff she puts on when she's going out for a big night with Lyle and wants to look like somebody no one around this house even recognizes. It's sort of scary.

But not as scary as that stuff would look on Sarah Fortemeyer.

"I'm doing my homework," I told her,

still not opening the door. In fact, I was wondering if there was a quick way of barricading my room so that I would be safe until my mom and Lyle got home.

Too late. The doorknob turned. I stared at the wall in front of me, determined not to turn around and look. I was pretty sure seeing Sarah Fortemeyer in one of my mom's weird boa things would stunt my growth.

For life.

"Look," Sarah said. She walked across the room to my desk and shoved her hand under my eyes, which I immediately closed. "I found twelve of them. There were a whole bunch out by the swing set."

Slowly, very slowly, I opened my eyes. In Sarah's hand were twelve dried-up worm carcasses. One of them was almost

torn in two, so it didn't count, but the others were in pristine condition.

"You found these by the swing set?" I asked her.

"Yeah," she said, dumping the worms on my notebook. "You know, where your mom threw out all those worms last year? The ones you gave her for . . . oh. Sorry. I bet most of them are just fine, though. I mean, there were hundreds of those suckers when she dumped them. So if I only found twelve, the rest are probably still just dandy, Andy."

I nodded. And felt like a dupe. Why hadn't I ever thought of looking by the swing set? It was a brilliant, maybe even a genius, idea.

I looked up at Sarah Fortemeyer with new respect. Well, I almost did. But just as I was about to communicate my scientific regard for her worm geniosity, I noticed she was wearing pink and purple feather earrings, two per ear.

There are not enough dried worms on the face of the Earth to make up for that.

chapter twelve

As of this morning, scientists everywhere can add Ben Robbins and Aretha
Timmons to the amazing list of famous
chemical reactions. This list includes,
among many other things, baking soda
and vinegar, which together produce
carbon dioxide gas, and diluted hydro-
chloric acid mixed up with sodium
sulfide, which makes a stinkazoid rotten-
egg smell in no time.

Now it includes Ben and Aretha.

By themselves they're just two ordinary human beings.

Together they are a Ben and Aretha Explosion.

This morning Mrs. Tuttle's class listened to the presidential candidates' speeches. I did not have high hopes, even with Aretha on the ticket. First of all, as the head speechwriter, I knew just how lousy Ben's speech was. When you are writing a speech at the same time your mom is standing behind you ranting and raving, well, it can be a little hard to concentrate.

I'd been sitting at my desk, chewing on my pencil, completely unable to find a good way to say "Ben is not as crazy as you think," when my mom burst into my room. She was wearing her bathrobe and had on this funny pink plastic cap she wears when she's going to take a shower but doesn't want to wash her hair.

Which is when it hit me: We'd completely forgotten about the mold samples getting jump-started in my mom's shower.

I was doomed.

"I'm not sure where you got the idea my shower stall is a science lab, buster, but you are sadly mistaken," my mom said, waving a hairbrush around in the air. Just because my mom is Miss No Spanking, Just Lots of Boring Lectures doesn't mean she won't make you nervous that maybe she's changed her mind. "Did you really think I was going to let you use my shower to grow mold?"

"We were going to take the mold out before you got back," I tried to explain.

"I guess I sort of forgot. Besides, it wasn't even mold. It was just potential mold."

My mom pointed the hairbrush at me. "Well, it's mold now, Mac."

"Really?" I couldn't believe it—our experiment had worked, at super warp speed! "That's great!"

My mom stared me down. She used her best *I am your mother and buy all your clothes and food and pay your doctors' bills and work hard each and every day and you are in so much trouble you can't even believe it* look.

"Your shower stall was kind of moldy already, Mom," I said, hoping to reason with her. "Really, a few more mold spores aren't going to make that big of a difference."

If my mom had been a cartoon character, this would have been the point where steam started coming out of her ears.

"I can't believe Sarah let you do this," she said, starting to pace back and forth across my room. "I always thought she was so responsible, but now I have to wonder."

I couldn't believe it. I had never heard my mother doubt the complete wonderfulness of Sarah Fortemeyer before. Were Sarah's days as Teenage Girl Space Alien babysitter numbered? Would we get a normal babysitter instead? Maybe we'd get one of those old lady babysitters who were always baking cookies and telling you to run along and watch TV.

I liked this idea. I liked it a lot. In fact, I sort of started daydreaming about it right then. The old lady babysitter would never wear purple clothes or feather earrings, and she would wear one of those sweaters with pockets. Pockets filled with candy. Lots of candy.

I sighed. Even with my mom steaming behind me, I was feeling sort of peaceful and relaxed, thinking about this new old lady babysitter tossing around peppermint patties and Hershey's Kisses left and right.

And then I remembered the worms.

All twelve of them, hunted down by Sarah Fortemeyer in the backyard. Eleven of them in pristine condition.

"Sarah didn't know anything about it," I told my mom. "Ben and I set up the experiment while she was putting Margaret to bed. We sort of snuck around her."

My mom harrumphed. And then she made me spend an hour washing out her shower stall with a scrubber and some stinky bleach solution, even though no mold was actually growing anywhere on the tiles in her shower stall, at least not mold that I personally was responsible for.

So anyway, by the time I got around to finishing the speech, I wasn't exactly at my most energetic best.

The second reason I didn't have high hopes was that as Ben's best friend, I knew just how bad Ben was at making speeches.

Third, as a human being alive on this planet, I knew that even with Aretha's help, Ben still had about a 0 percent chance of winning this election.

But here is the brilliant scheme Ben came up with: He convinced Mrs. Tuttle to let Aretha give his speech with him.

They would speak last, after Roland, Stacey, and Chester had all had their turns. I couldn't decide if this was a good or bad thing. On the one hand, by the time Ben and Aretha made their speech, everyone might be sick of speeches. But maybe because their speech was the last speech, it would be the speech everyone remembered.

Too bad it was such a lousy speech.

Fortunately, Roland Forth had a lousy speech too. The thing about Roland is that he is a hummer. Wherever he is— sitting at his desk, playing kickball during recess, or eating a peanut butter sandwich at lunch—he's always humming. Sometimes it's sort of funny, like when he is humming and kicking the kickball at the same time. Mostly, though, it's the most irritating thing that ever happened to you. Try taking a geography test while a kid in the third row of your class is humming "The Wheels on the Bus Go Round and Round" and you'll see what I mean.

What happened during Roland's speech is that he would say a sentence, and then he would hum a little. Sentence, hum, sentence, hum. After a while it was totally impossible to concentrate on what he was saying because you were too busy waiting for the humming to start again.

Next came Chester. I was afraid his speech would be so funny that people would just automatically vote for him right then and there, even though the election wasn't until Thursday. Chester, in my opinion, will be the hardest person to beat. Unlike Roland, he is normal; unlike Stacey, he is nice; and unlike

Ben, he would make a good president.

But what I thought could never happen in a million years happened. Chester gave an unfunny speech. You could tell he wanted everyone to see his serious side. I guess that's a problem for naturally funny people—nobody even knows they have a serious side.

The problem with Chester's serious side was it was sort of boring. He said a lot of stuff about rules he would make, like no spitting out gum in the water fountain, which he personally found really gross, and no do-overs in kickball just because the pitcher had rolled a bouncy pitch.

After Chester gave his speech, I looked around the classroom. Everybody's mouth was hanging open, like they were thinking, *When did the space aliens come trade out Chester's personality for the personality of the most boring person who ever lived?*

Stacey's speech was about good manners and respecting the teacher and getting more pizza parties. When she finished, all her friends chanted, "Go, Stacey! Go, Stacey!"

If she wins class president, I will be automatically transferring to another school.

When it was time for Ben to make his speech, Aretha came and stood beside him. What I didn't know is that they had worked up a routine. Ben didn't exactly give the speech. He had written it out on big poster sheets and illustrated each poster with cartoons. So the speech started with Ben holding out a poster with a picture of his face on it that said: HI, MY NAME IS BEN ROBBINS AND I

AM RUNNING FOR PRESIDENT OF MRS. TUTTLE'S FOURTH-GRADE CLASS.

Then Aretha stepped forward. "Why vote for Ben? That's a good question. It is a question I have asked myself many times, especially now that I am running for vice president on Ben's ticket. Here is the first good reason: You should vote for Ben because he was smart enough to ask me to be his vice president."

Ben pulled out another poster. This one had a picture of Aretha on it. Beneath the picture Ben had printed out, ARETHA TIMMONS IS MY VICE PRESIDENTIAL CANDIDATE. BESIDES BEING ONE OF THE SMARTEST PEOPLE IN OUR CLASS, SHE IS ORGANIZED AND FAIR.

Aretha nodded. "That's right, folks, a vote for Ben is also a vote for me. Now, let me tell you some other reasons to vote for Ben. He is a creative problem

solver. He thinks we need more snacks and a longer recess. He won an honorable mention in the fourth-grade science fair, which shows he is a good student."

The speech went on from there. Every point that Aretha made was illustrated in Ben's artistic-genius style. She said stuff in a way that made you think she was 100 percent correct. Even though the speech I had written was pretty boring, Aretha made it sound interesting. Ben's pictures almost made you feel like you were watching Saturday-morning cartoons.

You could tell just by looking around that people were starting to feel like a Ben and Aretha presidency would be a fun and exciting experience that they would want to be a part of. In fact, after the applause following the speech had died down, a bunch of kids went up to

Aretha and asked how they could help with the campaign.

I felt sort of famous just because Ben was my best friend.

"That was awesome!" I told him when he came back to his seat. "You guys did a great job!"

Instead of looking excited, though, Ben looked sort of worried. "What's wrong?" I asked him.

"I don't know," he said. "I guess when I was up there and everybody really liked what we were doing, it sort of felt like we were tricking them."

"Politics is a tricky business," I pointed out. I don't actually know what that

means. It's just something my dad says a lot during election years.

"I guess," Ben said. But he looked unhappy. "It's just, now if people vote for me, it'll be because of that speech."

"Isn't that the idea? You give a good speech, people vote for you."

"But what they liked is how we gave the speech," Ben said, chewing on a finger-nail. "Not what we said. I want them to vote for me and my ideas. Otherwise it's just some stupid popularity contest."

It had never occurred to me that Ben would actually care why people voted for him. I thought he just wanted their votes, for whatever reason, just so his dad would be happy that Ben was class president.

Scientifically speaking, it looked like the political process was turning Ben into a serious human being.

Which was a little frightening, if you want to know the truth.

Aretha leaned over and popped Ben on the arm with her pencil. "Don't look so glum, chum. I think we are going to win this election."

Ben nodded. "Yeah, I know," he said. "It's pretty cool."

But you could tell he didn't mean it.

chapter thirteen

On the bus home after school, I came up with three reasons Ben didn't seem very excited about everyone liking his speech so much.

1. He was worried that because he was running on the same ticket as Aretha, people in our class would think he wanted to marry her. This is a big problem with

even talking to a girl in fourth grade. Everyone thinks if a boy is halfway nice to a girl, he must be in love with her. Sometimes you end up being mean to girls you don't even hate just so no one gets the wrong idea.

2. He had suddenly realized that a successful career as a politician would make a serious dent in the amount of time he spent watching cartoons on TV in his pajamas.

3. For some reason he didn't really want his dad to come visit.

The third reason seemed pretty unlikely to me. So did the first reason, since Ben never acts like he cares all that much about what people think of him.

And the second reason was dumb, even for Ben.

So, scientifically speaking, I had no idea what was wrong with him.

When I got home, I checked my mold first thing, even before checking in with Sarah Fortemeyer, Teenage Girl Space Alien. It was just too exciting knowing there was a room full of slime mold in the house to worry about following the rules. Every great scientist has to go his own way, even if that means missing out on valuable fingernail polish viewing time.

We all have to make sacrifices in the name of science.

I have always loved my room. So far in my life I've lived in three houses, and in each house my room has been the best place for me to be. My latest room is the best room ever, especially since my mom has thrown up her hands and said I could decorate it any way I want to. In my last room my mom did this whole sailboat and teddy bear theme, and even though I was only six at the time, I knew it was dumb to have little teddy bears in sailor suits all over my wallpaper. I knew it was even dumber to have matching pajamas, but fortunately, I had a growth spurt and my mom couldn't find the same pajamas in a bigger size.

Now my walls are covered with posters. I have three solar system posters, one periodical table poster, which is all the chemical elements known to humankind in one simple-to-read chart, and a five-foot-tall poster of Albert Einstein with his hair sticking out all over the place. Everywhere I look, I find something awesome to look at. Not to mention that there are snacks, books, crumbs, and little messes everywhere.

And now there is mold.

I have never been so happy in my life.

I checked on my molds and took notes. The mold terrarium was looking pretty steamy, and inside the Cheerios had already started to wilt. No mold yet, but I figured it would only take a day or two more before it was a wonderland of mold spores in there. And while it would take another couple of weeks before my slime molds began growing, the yellow slime mold Ben and I had captured in the wild looked very happy in its new environment, which was a plastic bag on top of my bookshelf.

I thought about cleaning off my desk and my dresser so I could spread my mold samples out a little bit, but it was

clearly a job that would take at least two hours, maybe a week. I decided to call Ben instead and give him a mold update.

When he answered the phone, he still sounded unhappy.

"I don't get it," I said. "All you've been talking about for a whole week is winning this election. And now that it looks like you actually might do it, you're acting like your pet hamster died or something."

"I had a pet hamster once," Ben said. "It didn't die, though. It escaped."

"Did you get another one?"

"No, I just waited for the first one to come back. In fact, I'm still waiting."

"Where did you live when your hamster escaped?" I asked.

"Seattle," Ben said. "But they say animals sometimes track down their owners, even when their owners have moved hundreds, even thousands, of miles away."

Yeah, dogs maybe. One cat out of a million. But a hamster?

I don't think so.

"So, did you call your dad to tell him what a great job you and Aretha did today?" I asked, keeping my hamster thoughts to myself.

"Nope," Ben said. "There's nothing to tell him about. I've decided to drop out of the race."

I couldn't believe it. "Are you crazy? You could win it, Ben. People thought your speech was really cool."

"No, they thought Aretha was really cool," Ben said. "I think she's really cool too. And she's smart and organized, just like your speech said. She ought to be president, not me. She'd be the best one out of everybody."

"But what about your dad coming to visit you if you win? What about pay-per-view movies and pizza?"

"There's pizza in Seattle," Ben said. "I'll just go visit him there, same as always."

I didn't know what to say. It wasn't like Ben to be so, well, reasonable. I mean, Aretha *would* make a great president. And he and his dad could definitely order pizza and watch movies in Seattle.

Still, it's hard to see somebody's dream die, even if the dream was sort of dumb to begin with.

"Hey, some of our mold's starting to grow," I said, trying to cheer him up. "The stuff growing on the bread is this really interesting shade of blue. Sort of like a scab."

"Scabs are gray, or else purple," Ben said. "I've never seen a blue scab in my life."

"Imagine mixing the purple and gray," I told him. "That's the sort of blue I'm talking about."

"Yeah, I can sort of see what you're saying," Ben said, and by the way his voice sounded, I could tell he could see it in his head. That is one of the good things about having an artistic genius for your best friend. They're very good at imagining stuff.

"You want to hear about the mold terrarium?" I asked.

"Yeah," Ben said. He was starting to sound a little happier. "Is the tomato totally grossazoid or what?"

If you ever have to cheer somebody up, try talking to them about mold.

Scientifically speaking, it works 100 percent of the time.

chapter fourteen

It turns out that Mrs. Wanda Patino, principal of Woodbrook Elementary School, is not a big fan of mold.

"In the basement of my school?" she said after I'd given her my Amazing Mold presentation, complete with illustrations and fun facts. "You want to grow mold in the basement of my school?"

"Well, it's kind of everybody's school," I pointed out. "And Mr. Reid said it would be okay."

"You want to grow mold in the basement of my school?" she asked again.

Scientifically speaking, this conversation was starting to get a little boring.

"It's a science project," I told her. "It's educational. It's probably the most educational thing any kid will do in this school all year. And our school would be the only school around for miles with its own mold museum. You might win an award for Most Scientific Principal or something."

Mrs. Patino just shook her head. I could tell I was not doing a very good job of convincing her of the wonderfulness of mold.

"Mac, I'm impressed by your initiative here," she said after about two more minutes of head shaking. "But there are health codes we have to think about.

Under the wrong conditions mold can be a very dangerous thing."

"You're thinking about a different kind of mold," I insisted. "The kind that gets inside buildings and makes people sick. That's not the kind of mold I'm growing. Most of the molds I'm growing are slime molds. And they're all in covered containers."

"I'm sorry, Mac," Mrs. Patino said. She stood up and walked around to the front of her desk. "But I think I'd have a hard time convincing the school superintendent that your mold museum was anything but a health hazard."

I knew there wasn't any use in arguing anymore. You can always tell with adults. When they're finished with a topic once and for all, they get this little smile on their face like, *I win, and no*

offense, but there's nothing you can do about it, so now I'm going to go eat some disgusting snack like green olives with pimentos stuck in them, if you don't mind.

When I got out of Mrs. Patino's office, lunch was almost over, and everybody in my class was on the playground. After I put my posters and my mold samples back in Mrs. Tuttle's room, I went outside and found Ben over by the jungle gym, planting some sticks in the ground.

"You can't make trees grow that way, you know," I told him.

"I'm not growing trees," he said. "I'm visualizing."

"Visualizing what?"

"This scene I'm trying to draw in 'Derek the Destroyer Meets the Amazon Volleyball Players.' The amazons are chasing Derek through the jungle, and there's going to be this trap where a net falls down from some trees. Anyway, for some reason I've been having a hard time visualizing how the trap works."

I sat down next to Ben. I was visualizing my hard work flushed down the toilet. I was visualizing a whole bunch of mold all dressed up with no place to go. In a few short days I had created a universe of mold—blue mold, green mold, snowy white mold, and speckled black mold—and for what? Instead of going into a museum to be admired by millions—or at least by the entire fourth grade of Woodbrook Elementary School— it would go into the trash.

Well, not the slime mold. The slime mold was staying in my room.

"Hey, Mac, didn't we have a deal?"

I looked up. Aretha was standing in front of me. She had her hand on her hip.

"If I recall correctly, you owe me some penicillin mold," she went on. "My troop meets tomorrow. It would be nice to be able to make the penicillin before then so I can get my badge."

I couldn't believe it. In all the excitement of the last few days, the big speech and the big presentation and now the big, huge, disappointing letdown of no mold museum, I'd forgotten all about the penicillium mold growing in our bathroom closet.

"I can bring what I have tomorrow," I told her. "You know it's not going to be like some pink bubble-gum-tasting stuff in a childproof bottle, right? I mean, I grew the mold. I don't exactly know how to squeeze out the mold juice and turn it into medicine. I guess that would be your part of the process."

"Mold juice?" Aretha said. "Nobody ever said anything about mold juice."

"That's what penicillin comes from," I said. "Mold juice."

"I don't know if the Girl Scouts will like that," Aretha said.

"If they're like everybody else, they'll hate it," I said. "They'll find it disgusting and gross and a health hazard. But it's just mold. It's part of nature's recycling project. You can use it for medicine or for blue cheese. What could be so wrong with it?"

"I love blue cheese," Aretha said. "At least, I love blue cheese salad dressing."

"It's mold," I said with a sigh. "Just good old misunderstood mold."

Aretha looked at me. "Let me guess.

Mrs. Patino said no to your mold museum idea."

I nodded.

"Hey, you didn't tell me that," Ben said. "That's really stinkazoid."

"She said mold is a health hazard," I said.

"Blue cheese is a health hazard?" Aretha folded her arms over her chest. "I don't think so."

Then she turned to Ben. "Maybe we should make this part of our campaign. 'A vote for Ben and Aretha is a vote for mold!' If we get elected, we could get everybody to sign a petition, and then Mrs. Patino would have to let Mac have his mold museum."

"Um," Ben said. He cleared his throat. "Um, there's something I need to tell you."

Aretha eyed him suspiciously. "You have a problem with mold too?"

"Uh, no, that's not it," Ben said. "It's just that I've decided not to run for president."

"What? Why not?"

Ben looked at his sticks. "Because I think you should be president. You'd do a lot better job than I would."

"But I don't want to be president," Aretha said. "I don't even want to be vice president. All I want is twenty merit badges by December."

"If you didn't want to be vice president, why did you agree to run on my ticket?" Ben asked.

"Because I didn't think you would win, quite frankly," Aretha said. "Besides, I needed some help making penicillin, remember?"

"But now I probably am going to win," Ben said. "Only, the only reason I'm probably going to win is because of you. When you and I made that speech, everybody saw that you're, like, a leader or something. I'm just an artist."

"I do have natural leadership abilities, it's true," Aretha admitted. "But I do not have political drive. The only time I really got excited about the election was when we made that speech together. Then it didn't seem like politics. It seemed like fun."

"It's like Ben has the drive and you have the skills," I said. "And together you make a team that people want to vote for."

BIG CHEESE

"We do make a good team," Aretha agreed. "It's not something I would have predicted, but I have to admit it's a fact. And I guess after we made that speech, I did start to feel like being vice president would be interesting. Although, frankly, I would make a better president than vice president. Ben's right about that."

A flash went off in my head. "So why don't you switch?" I asked.

"Switch what?" Ben asked.

"Why doesn't Aretha run for president and you run for vice president? Because Aretha would be a great president, which everybody knew the minute you guys started making your speech, including Aretha. But you'd make a good vice president, Ben. You're the one who would bring creativity and energy to your administration."

Ben and Aretha looked at each other. They nodded.

A switch. What a brilliant concept.

Really, sometimes I amaze myself with my own geniosity.

🔔 chapter fifteen

The next genius idea came from Ben.

Which sort of surprised me, if you want to know the truth.

I mean, he's a great artist and every-thing, but his ideas aren't usually so hot. Like the time he decided to draw an entire Derek the Destroyer story on his bedroom walls.

Using permanent markers.

Specifically speaking, using Midnight Black permanent markers, which can

never ever be washed off, even if your mom has a total fit when she sees what you've done.

That's a pretty typical Ben idea.

His genius idea came after his dad's visit, after Ben and Aretha won the election on Thursday morning. Even though Ben was only vice president and not president, his dad still flew all the way from Seattle.

It turns out that Ben's dad thinks being vice president will look almost as good on Ben's résumé as being president.

Not that Ben has a résumé.

To be honest, I'm not even sure Ben knows what a résumé is.

When Ben's dad came to visit him the weekend after the election, he gave Ben his old video camcorder, since he'd just gotten a new mini-DV camcorder. He told Ben if he wanted to be an artist so much, he should at least be a video artist so he could make some money. Ben said he would think about it, which made his dad happy.

One day Ben's dad will accept him for being the comic-book artist genius that he is. But for now Ben is having a lot of fun taking videos of everything that moves.

Even stuff that moves really, really slowly.

Ever watched a video of slime mold?

Now you can, every day at lunch, in the basement of Woodbrook Elementary School.

Mr. Reid provides the snacks.

Not that too many of the people watching the video have really felt like eating snacks. I like to think this is because they are so in love with the slime mold that they are too enraptured to even think about eating.

But I'm pretty sure it's because they're grossed out.

It took three weeks to make the video. Every day Ben would come over to my house, and we would set up bright lights and film the slime mold race.

From day to day it was hard to see any progress. But when you looked at three weeks of tape all run together, you could really see the molds moving.

It's possible that slime mold racing will be the next big trend at Woodbrook Elementary.

Ben also videotaped me telling all the wondrous facts about mold, what it is and what it does. And Lyle lent me his digital camera so I could take lots of pictures of the mold I grew at home, as well as mold I found out in the woods and other places, such as my refrigerator and Ben's shower. I put the pictures into a slide show that Mr. Reid shows on his computer for anybody that's interested.

You will be happy to hear that a lot of people are very interested.

I think one reason mold has caught on in a big way at my school is that the first week we set up the exhibit, it was rainy. So after lunch you had the choice of being bored out of your mind playing hangman in Mrs. Tuttle's classroom, or going down to the basement and watching Mold TV.

I don't know one single fourth grader who would say no to a little TV watching during school hours.

Now that people know I know how to grow slime mold, I am getting a lot of orders. So me, Ben, and Aretha are thinking about starting a business.

"Maybe we should start a campaign to make slime mold our official classroom mascot," Aretha said this morning at recess. We were sitting on the jungle gym, which had sort of become our meeting spot for discussing fourth-grade politics and mold ideas.

"I could design slime mold T-shirts," Ben said. "We could sell them to raise money for a class pizza party."

"And if a slime mold is our class mascot, our business would really take off," I said. "Everybody would want their own slime mold to show their class spirit."

"And if we have a successful business, I will earn the Business-Wise merit badge," said Aretha. "Which means I only have seven more to go to meet my goal of twenty by December, since I got my health merit badge last week."

Aretha ended up using her mom's blender to get the penicillin juice out of the penicillium mold, in case you were wondering.

Her mom is making her buy a new blender. With her own money.

As I walked home from the bus stop, my brain was

full of ideas for a successful mold business. Besides selling slime molds, we could sell Grow Your Own Mold kits, which would include bread, an eyedropper, some mold spores, and instructions. We could also give tours of my refrigerator, for a small fee.

Sarah Fortemeyer, Teenage Girl Space Alien, was sitting at the kitchen table polishing her fingernails when I got home. Today she was trying out various shades of purple.

I nearly broke out in hives just watching her.

"You know, Macky Mac, I've been thinking about it," Sarah said, "and I've decided that we have a lot in common."

I staggered backward a few steps.

This was the meanest thing Sarah Fortemeyer had ever said to me.

"For instance, we both like to experiment," she said, waving her fingers at me. "You like to experiment with mold, I like to experiment with fingernail polish. Today I have ten different shades of purple, from Greatest Grape to Violently Violet."

I checked my arm. I was pretty sure I could see little red dots popping up as Sarah spoke.

"Today I think I have accomplished one of my most significant experiments to date," Sarah continued, standing up. "If you'll follow me, you will witness an amazing transformation."

Sarah began walking toward the stairs. I felt my stomach grow cold with fear.

She was heading toward my room.

I followed behind her, slowly. Very slowly.

As slowly as a slime mold, only slower.

"Come on, Mac!" Sarah called to me from the top of the steps. "You're really going to like this. One hundred percent guaranteed."

I slimed my way up the stairs. When I reached the doorway to my room, I closed my eyes.

I had always really liked my room. The comfortableness of it. The lived-in quality of it. The sheer sloppy Big Mac–attack factor of it.

I knew when I opened my eyes, that would all be gone.

"I checked with your mom to see if this would be okay," Sarah said. Her voice sounded like it was coming from inside my room. My eyes were still closed, so I didn't know for sure. "Since I'm taking a carpentry class in school, I do have the necessary skills needed for this sort of project."

Sarah Fortemeyer, Teenage Girl Space Alien from the Planet of Really Pink Stuff, was taking a carpentry class? My eyes popped open from the sheer surprise of this idea.

And that's when I saw what she had done to my room.

She had turned it into a mold museum.

She had mounted three shelves to the wall above my desk, and three more above the head of my bed. My mold samples, which now number thirty-seven, lined the shelves.

"I . . . I can't believe it," I stammered. "This is incredible."

Sarah shrugged. "Yeah, well, I felt bad when I heard they wouldn't let you display your mold at school. I know

how much it means to you."

I sat on my bed, stunned. Why hadn't I thought of this? A mold museum in my very own room!

It was like a dream come true.

"I guess you don't want to give me a hug or something, just to say thanks, do you?" Sarah asked.

I am a scientist. I do not hug Teenage Girl Space Aliens.

However, I do shake their hands when necessary.

So now I have decided to revise my goal list for Mrs. Tuttle's class. Here are my new fourth-grade goals:

1. To discover the reason a person would break out in hives just from looking at purple fingernail polish

2. To use Ben and Aretha's political influence to make Mr. Reid the principal of Woodbrook Elementary School, since he is the main adult genius there, as far as I can tell

3. To use the newly constructed Phineas L. MacGuire Museum of Mold to educate people about the many wonders of mold and maybe even make a little extra money by charging a small admission fee

I was thinking I could use the extra money to build a chemistry lab in my closet.

I would definitely be the best fourth-grade scientist ever if I had a chemistry lab in my closet.

Just don't tell my mom, okay?

MAC'S SCIENCE

EXPERIMENTS

HOW TO GROW PENICILLIN

What you'll need:

- a lemon wedge
- dust
- a plastic bag
- water
- an eyedropper
- a clean, empty
  milk carton

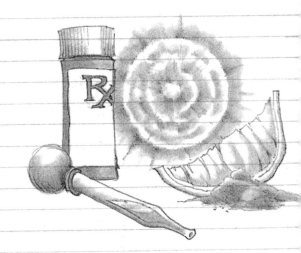

How to do it:

Wipe the lemon wedge across a dusty surface to
collect dust on it. When you've collected a sufficient
amount of dust, drop the lemon wedge into a plastic
bag and add five drops of water with an eyedropper.
Then plop the bag into the milk carton and seal the
carton. After several days, mold should appear on
the lemon wedge.

So what happened?

The mold that appears on the lemon wedge is called PENICILLIUM. It's a mold that really likes citrus fruits such as lemons, limes, and grapefruits. As it grows, a liquid called PENICILLIN is produced. If you were working in a fancy science lab, you could transform this liquid penicillin into medicine—penicillin is an antibiotic used to treat sick people.

HOW TO MAKE A MOLD TERRARIUM

What you'll need:

- a plastic or glass container, such as a used, clean mayonnaise jar, with a lid
- bits and pieces of food (but no meat or fish), such as grapes, bread, cheese, and veggies
- water

How to do it:

Put the food in the jar. Spread it out so it's not all piled on top of each other.

Spray or mist water over the food and seal the jar up tight. Label your jar so no one mistakes it for a snack (!) and put it in an out-of-the-way spot. After four or five days (maybe sooner) you'll begin to see all sorts of mold growing on the food. Let it rot to your heart's delight (or for as long as your mom can stand it).

So what happened?

Mold loves moisture and it loves to eat. Unlike other plants, mold can't make its own food, so it has to find it. Mold breaks down its food by producing chemicals that make the food rot so that the mold can eat it. Yum!

Please note: When you're done with your mold experiment, don't open the jar and let the mold spores escape. They can be harmful to breathe. So dump that mold in the trash—you can always make more.

HOW TO GROW SLIME MOLD

What you'll need:

- rotting tree bark
- paper towels
- water
- plastic container
- plastic wrap

How to do it:

Grab some rotting bark from your backyard or a tree near your school. Put a paper towel at the bottom of a plastic container, put the bark on top of the paper towel, and cover the bark with water. Cover the container with plastic wrap. The following day, dump out the water and re-cover the container. Make sure the paper towels stay damp throughout the process. Wait a few weeks and you should see some lovely slime crawling across your bark. You can also try this experiment with dead leaves or rotting wood. If slime doesn't grow on your first sample, try bark from different trees and see which ones are the real slime magnets.

So what happened?

Slime mold loves tree bark because as the bark rots, pieces of it get loose and trap moisture. And as we know, mold loves moisture. By creating a moist environment for your bark, you create excellent conditions for slime mold to thrive.